POWER OF MONEY

Dr. Maxwell Shimba

Copyright © 2024 – Dr. Maxwell Shimba
All rights reserved. No portion of this book may be reproduced, stored in a retrieval system, or transmitted in any form or by any means – electronics, mechanical, photocopy, recording, scanning, or other – except for brief quotations in critical reviews or articles, without the prior written permission of the publisher.

Published in Manhattan, New York by Shimba Publishing, LLC.

Shimba Publishing, LLC
Printed in the United States of America

First Printing Edition 2024

TABLE OF CONTENTS

Introduction v
The Multifaceted Influence of Money v
The Psychology of the Power of Money x
Chapter 1 1
The Genesis of Wealth 1
Chapter 02 5
The Psychology of Prosperity 5
Chapter 03 10
The Power of Money Creation 10
Chapter 04 17
The Power of Money to Create Inequality and Wealth 17
Chapter 05 24
The Power of Money to Wreak Devastation 24
Chapter 06 31
The Power of International Money 31
Chapter 07 39
The Economic Engine 39
Chapter 08 44
The Pursuit of Wealth and Its Shadows 44
Chapter 09 49
The Pathways to Wealth 49
Chapter 10 55
Money and Power 55
Chapter 11 61
The Battlefields of Global Finance 61
Chapter 12 67
From Rags to Riches 67

Chapter 13	73
The Hidden Costs of Economic Growth	73
Chapter 14	79
The Disruptive Power of Cryptocurrencies	79
Chapter 15	86
The Future of Finance	86
Conclusion	92

INTRODUCTION

THE MULTIFACETED INFLUENCE OF MONEY

Money, often described as the lifeblood of modern economies, is a force that permeates every aspect of our lives. From facilitating everyday transactions to shaping global geopolitics, its influence is vast and complex. As a medium of exchange, a store of value, and a unit of account, money's roles are foundational to the functioning of societies. However, its power extends far beyond these basic economic functions, impacting our psychology, social structures, and even our ethical frameworks.

A Historical Perspective

The history of money is as old as civilization itself. From the earliest barter systems to the creation of digital currencies, the evolution of money reflects humanity's ongoing quest for more efficient and reliable means of trade and value storage. Ancient coins, medieval banking innovations, and modern financial markets each tell a story of how societies have adapted their monetary systems to meet changing needs and circumstances. Understanding this history is crucial to appreciating the full scope of money's power and its role in shaping human progress.

Economic Growth and Development

One of the most apparent powers of money is its ability to drive economic growth and development. Access to capital enables businesses to expand, innovate, and create jobs, fostering a cycle of growth that lifts living standards and reduces poverty. Investments in infrastructure, education, and technology are all made possible through the mobilization of financial resources. However, the benefits of economic growth are not always evenly distributed, leading to significant wealth disparities and social tensions.

The Psychology of Money

Money also wields significant psychological influence. It can evoke a wide range of emotions, from security and contentment to anxiety and greed. The way individuals perceive and manage money often reflects their values, aspirations, and fears. Financial decisions are not made in a vacuum; they are influenced by cognitive biases, emotional states, and social pressures. The psychological aspects of money highlight the deep connections between our financial behaviors and our mental well-being.

Social and Political Dynamics

Beyond individual and economic impacts, money plays a crucial role in shaping social and political dynamics. It can empower communities and drive social change, but it can also entrench inequalities and corrupt political systems. Wealth concentration in the hands of a few can lead to disproportionate influence over policy and governance, undermining democratic processes and exacerbating social divides. Conversely, equitable access to financial resources can promote social justice and enhance collective well-being.

Technological Transformations

The digital age has ushered in unprecedented changes in how we think about and use money. Cryptocurrencies, blockchain technology, and fintech innovations are challenging traditional financial systems and creating new opportunities and risks. These technological advancements promise greater financial inclusion and efficiency but also raise questions about regulation, security, and the future of money itself. As we navigate these changes, it is essential to consider how they reshape our economic and social landscapes.

Ethical Considerations

The power of money also brings with it ethical dilemmas. The pursuit of profit can lead to behaviors that harm individuals, communities, and the environment. From labor exploitation to environmental degradation, the negative consequences of financial activities often reflect deeper moral and ethical issues. Addressing these challenges requires a commitment to responsible financial practices and a broader understanding of the true value of money in contributing to human flourishing.

Towards a Balanced Perspective

As we explore the power of money, it is important to adopt a balanced perspective that recognizes both its potential benefits and its inherent risks. Money can be a force for good, driving progress and improving lives, but it can also lead to destructive outcomes if misused or misunderstood. By examining the multifaceted influence of money, we can develop a more nuanced understanding of its role in our world and make more informed decisions about how to harness its power for the greater good.

Conclusion

This book aims to provide a comprehensive examination of the power of money from various perspectives, including its historical evolution, economic impact, psychological influence, social dynamics, technological transformations, and ethical implications. Through this exploration, we hope to shed light on the complex and often contradictory nature of money, offering insights that can help individuals, businesses, and policymakers navigate the financial challenges and opportunities of the modern world.

THE PSYCHOLOGY OF THE POWER OF MONEY

The Psychological Influence of Money

Money is more than just a medium of exchange or a store of value; it is a powerful psychological force that influences human behavior, emotions, and decision-making. The way individuals perceive, manage, and react to money can reveal deep insights into their motivations, values, and mental states. This chapter delves into the psychology of the power of money, exploring how it shapes our lives, relationships, and societal structures.

Perceptions of Wealth and Success

1. Symbol of Success:

   - In many cultures, money is a primary indicator of success and social status. Individuals often equate financial wealth with personal achievement and prestige. This perception drives behaviors such as the pursuit of high-paying careers, the acquisition of luxury goods, and the display of wealth.

2. Security and Stability:

- Money also represents security and stability. Financial resources provide a safety net against unforeseen circumstances, such as medical emergencies, job loss, or economic downturns. The desire for financial security can motivate individuals to save, invest, and plan for the future.

3. Self-Worth and Identity:

- For some, money is closely tied to their self-worth and identity. Financial success can boost self-esteem and provide a sense of accomplishment, while financial struggles may lead to feelings of inadequacy and failure. This psychological association can significantly impact one's mental health and overall well-being.

The Psychological Impact of Financial Stress

1. Anxiety and Depression:

- Financial stress is a major contributor to anxiety and depression. Worries about debt, bills, and financial obligations can create a constant state of tension and fear. Chronic financial stress can affect physical health, leading to issues such as insomnia, headaches, and high blood pressure.

2. Relationship Strain:

- Money is a common source of conflict in relationships. Disagreements over spending, saving, and financial priorities can strain partnerships and lead to resentment. Financial problems are a leading cause of divorce, highlighting the significant impact of money on personal relationships.

3. Decision-Making and Risk-Taking:

- Financial stress can influence decision-making processes, often leading to risk-averse or overly cautious behavior. Conversely, some individuals may engage in risky financial behaviors, such as gambling or speculative investments, in an attempt to alleviate financial pressures quickly.

Behavioral Economics: Understanding Financial Choices

1. Cognitive Biases:

- Cognitive biases affect how individuals make financial decisions. For example, the availability heuristic can cause people to overestimate the likelihood of financial success based on recent examples, while the loss aversion bias leads individuals to fear losses more than they value gains.

2. Mental Accounting:

- Mental accounting is the tendency to categorize and treat money differently depending on its source or intended use. For instance, people may spend a tax refund more freely than regular income, viewing it as "extra" money. This behavior can influence budgeting, saving, and spending habits.

3. Anchoring and Adjustment:

- The anchoring effect occurs when individuals rely too heavily on the first piece of information they encounter (the "anchor") when making decisions. In financial contexts, this can impact everything from negotiating salaries to setting prices for goods and services.

The Role of Financial Socialization

1. Family Influence:

- Financial behaviors and attitudes are often shaped by family upbringing. Parents' attitudes toward money, spending habits, and financial decision-making practices can significantly influence their children's financial behaviors and beliefs.

2. Cultural Norms:

- Cultural norms and values also play a crucial role in shaping financial behavior. Different cultures have varying attitudes towards saving, spending, debt, and wealth accumulation. Understanding these cultural influences can provide insights into diverse financial behaviors.

3. Financial Education:

- Financial education and literacy are essential for making informed financial decisions. Lack of financial knowledge can lead to poor money management, increased debt, and financial stress. Promoting financial literacy through education and accessible resources can empower individuals to manage their finances more effectively.

The Emotional Drivers of Financial Behavior

1. Fear and Greed:

- Fear and greed are powerful emotions that drive financial markets and individual behavior. Fear can lead to panic selling and market crashes, while greed can fuel speculative bubbles and risky investments. Understanding these emotional drivers is crucial for managing financial behavior and market dynamics.

2. Instant Gratification:

- The tendency for instant gratification can impact financial behavior, leading individuals to prioritize short-term rewards over long-term goals. Impulsive spending and insufficient savings are common consequences of the desire for immediate satisfaction.

3. Status and Competition:

- The desire for social status and competition can drive financial behavior, leading individuals to spend money to "keep up with the Joneses." This behavior can result in financial overextension and debt, as individuals prioritize appearances over financial stability.

Strategies for Managing the Psychological Impact of Money

1. Mindful Spending and Saving:

- Practicing mindful spending and saving involves being aware of one's financial habits and making intentional choices that align with long-term goals. This approach can reduce impulsive behaviors and promote financial well-being.

2. Setting Financial Goals:

- Setting clear and achievable financial goals can provide direction and motivation. Goals should be specific, measurable, attainable, relevant, and time-bound (SMART) to ensure progress and accountability.

3. Seeking Professional Advice:

- Financial advisors and counselors can provide valuable guidance and support in managing finances. Professional advice can help individuals develop effective financial strategies, address financial stress, and make informed decisions.

4. Building Financial Resilience:

- Building financial resilience involves creating a financial cushion to handle unexpected expenses and economic downturns. Emergency savings, insurance, and diversified investments are key components of financial resilience.

Accordingly, the Psychological Power of Money extends far beyond its economic functions, deeply influencing psychological and emotional aspects of human life. Understanding the psychology of money can help individuals make better financial decisions, manage stress, and achieve greater financial well-being. By recognizing the complex interplay between money, behavior, and emotions, we can harness the power of money to enhance our lives and contribute to a more financially healthy and resilient society.

DR. MAXWELL SHIMBA

CHAPTER 1

THE GENESIS OF WEALTH

The Birth of Exchange

In the earliest human societies, trade was the fundamental method of obtaining goods and services. The barter system, where people exchanged items of perceived equal value, was the first form of economic transaction. However, barter had its limitations; it required a double coincidence of wants, meaning both parties had to have what the other desired.

The Evolution of Barter Systems

As societies grew more complex, the inefficiencies of barter became apparent. To address these challenges, early civilizations began to use commodities that had intrinsic value and were universally accepted. Livestock, grain, and even shells became early forms of money due to their durability, divisibility, and portability.

The Advent of Metal Money

Around 600 BCE, the Lydians, a people from modern-day Turkey, are credited with creating the first coins. These coins were made from electrum, a naturally occurring alloy of gold and silver. The standardization of coins revolutionized trade, as they were easier to carry and verify compared to barter items. Coins became symbols of wealth and power, enabling the rise of economies and empires.

The Role of Money in Ancient Civilizations

The use of coins spread rapidly across ancient civilizations. In Greece, money facilitated the development of markets and democracy, while in Rome, it underpinned the vast economic networks of the Roman Empire. Money allowed these societies to collect taxes, pay soldiers, and build infrastructure, fostering growth and stability.

Paper Money and Banking Systems

The Chinese were the pioneers of paper money during the Tang Dynasty (618–907 CE). Paper money addressed the limitations of metal coins, such as scarcity and weight. The concept of paper money eventually spread to the Islamic world and Europe, where it laid the groundwork for modern banking systems.

In medieval Europe, the establishment of banks transformed economic transactions. Banks offered services such as loans, deposits, and the issuance of promissory notes, which functioned as early forms of paper money. The Medici family in Italy became prominent bankers, financing trade and political ventures across Europe.

The Profound Impact of Money on Human Societies

The evolution of money from barter systems to coins and currency had a profound impact on human societies. It facilitated the rise of complex economies, enabling large-scale trade and commerce. The money allowed for the specialization of labor, where individuals could focus on specific tasks and trade their goods and services for others.

Furthermore, money became a tool for social organization and control. Governments could levy taxes, fund armies, and implement public works, solidifying their power and influence. Money also influenced cultural and intellectual developments, as it funded artistic endeavors, education, and scientific advancements.

Conclusion: The Foundation of Modern Economies

The genesis of wealth through the evolution of money laid the foundation for modern economies. From the barter systems of ancient times to the sophisticated financial instruments of today, money remains a central pillar of human society. Understanding its history helps us appreciate its role in shaping civilizations and its continuing influence on our lives.

In the following chapters, we will explore the various facets of money, from its psychological impact to its role in power dynamics and prospects. The journey of money is a testament to human ingenuity and its relentless pursuit of progress and prosperity.

CHAPTER 02

THE PSYCHOLOGY OF PROSPERITY

The Mind and Money

Money, though a tangible object, holds immense psychological power. It affects our emotions, decisions, and behaviors in profound ways. Understanding the psychological aspects of money can shed light on why individuals pursue wealth, how they manage financial resources and the emotional consequences that come with financial success or failure.

Perceptions of Wealth

How individuals perceive wealth varies widely based on cultural, social, and personal factors. For some, wealth is a measure of success and self-worth, while for others, it represents security and freedom. These perceptions influence financial behaviors and priorities. For instance, those who see wealth as a status symbol might spend more on luxury items, while those who view it as a means to security might prioritize saving and investing.

The Psychology of Spending

Spending habits reveal much about an individual's psychological relationship with money. The act of purchasing can provide a temporary sense of happiness or satisfaction, often referred to as retail therapy. However, impulsive spending can lead to financial stress and regret. Understanding the triggers for spending, such as emotional states or social pressures, can help individuals make more mindful financial decisions.

Saving and Investing: The Long-Term Perspective

Saving and investing require a different psychological approach than spending. They involve delaying gratification for future benefits. The ability to save and invest effectively often correlates with traits such as self-discipline, foresight, and risk tolerance. Psychological factors like optimism and confidence can also impact investment decisions, sometimes leading to overconfidence and risky financial behaviors.

Financial Decision-Making

The field of behavioral economics explores how psychological factors influence financial decisions. Cognitive biases, such as the anchoring effect, where individuals rely too heavily on the first piece of information encountered, or the herd mentality, where people follow the actions of a larger group, can lead to irrational financial choices. Recognizing these biases can help individuals make more rational and informed financial decisions.

The Emotional Toll of Money

Money can be a significant source of stress and anxiety. Financial pressures, such as debt, unemployment, or inadequate savings, can lead to emotional distress and impact mental health. On the other hand, financial stability and prosperity can enhance well-being, providing a sense of security and peace of mind. It's essential to address the emotional aspects of money to maintain overall health and happiness.

Wealth and Happiness

While money can contribute to happiness, it is not a direct or guaranteed path to well-being. Research suggests that after a certain point, additional wealth has a diminishing return on happiness. The quality of relationships, personal fulfillment, and a sense of purpose often play more significant roles in long-term happiness than financial wealth alone.

The Role of Financial Education

Financial literacy is crucial for managing money effectively. A lack of financial knowledge can lead to poor financial decisions and increased stress. Educating individuals about budgeting, investing, and planning for the future can empower them to take control of their financial lives and reduce anxiety related to money.

Cultural Influences on Financial Behavior

Cultural norms and values significantly impact financial behaviors. Different cultures have varying attitudes toward saving, spending, and investing. For instance, some cultures emphasize communal wealth and support, while others prioritize individual financial success. Understanding these cultural influences can provide insights into diverse financial behaviors and practices.

The Impact of Technology on Financial Psychology

Technology has transformed how we manage and perceive money. Digital banking, online shopping, and financial apps have made money management more accessible but also more complex. The ease of online transactions can encourage impulsive spending, while access to financial information can help individuals make more informed decisions. Balancing technology's benefits and challenges is essential for healthy financial behavior.

Conclusion: The Mindset of Prosperity

The psychology of prosperity encompasses a wide range of emotional and cognitive factors that influence how individuals perceive, manage, and are affected by money. By understanding these psychological aspects, individuals can develop healthier financial habits, make more informed decisions, and ultimately achieve a more balanced and fulfilling relationship with wealth. In the next chapter, we will explore how money drives economies, shaping societies and influencing global dynamics.

CHAPTER 03

THE POWER OF MONEY CREATION

The Mechanics and Impact of Money Creation

Money creation is a fundamental process that drives economic activity and influences financial stability. Understanding how money is created, who controls its creation, and the impact it has on economies and societies is crucial to comprehending the broader dynamics of financial systems. This chapter delves into the mechanisms of money creation, its power, and its implications for global economic health.

The Basics of Money Creation

1. The Role of Central Banks:

   - Central banks, such as the Federal Reserve in the United States, the European Central Bank (ECB), and the

Bank of Japan, play a pivotal role in money creation. They regulate the money supply through monetary policy tools like interest rates, open market operations, and reserve requirements.

- Central banks can create money directly by purchasing government securities or other financial assets, a process known as quantitative easing (QE). This injects liquidity into the financial system, encouraging lending and investment.

2. Fractional Reserve Banking:

- Commercial banks also create money through the process of fractional reserve banking. When banks receive deposits, they are required to keep only a fraction of those deposits as reserves and can lend out the remainder. The money lent out then gets deposited in other banks, which can lend out a portion of those deposits, creating a multiplier effect.

- This system amplifies the money supply based on the reserve ratio set by the central bank. For example, with a 10% reserve ratio, a $1,000 deposit can theoretically create up to $10,000 in total money supply through successive rounds of lending and depositing.

The Impact of Money Creation on Economies

1. Stimulating Economic Growth:

   - Money creation can stimulate economic growth by increasing the availability of credit. When businesses and consumers have access to affordable loans, they are more likely to invest in new projects, expand operations, and spend on goods and services. This boost in economic activity can lead to higher employment and overall economic prosperity.

2. Controlling Inflation:

   - While money creation can spur growth, it must be carefully managed to avoid inflation. When too much money chases too few goods, prices rise, leading to inflation. Central banks use interest rates and other tools to balance money creation with inflation control. For instance, raising interest rates can reduce borrowing and slow down money creation, helping to keep inflation in check.

3. Addressing Economic Crises:

   - During economic crises, central banks often engage in aggressive money creation to stabilize the economy. For example, during the 2008 financial crisis and the COVID-19 pandemic, central banks implemented large-scale QE programs to support financial markets, ensure liquidity, and promote economic recovery.

The Power and Controversy of Money Creation

1. Sovereign Debt and Deficits:

- Governments often rely on money creation to finance deficits and manage sovereign debt. While this can provide short-term relief, excessive reliance on money creation can lead to long-term economic problems, such as hyperinflation or loss of confidence in the currency.

2. Wealth Distribution:

- Money creation can affect wealth distribution. Quantitative easing and other monetary policies often lead to asset price inflation, benefiting those who own stocks, real estate, and other financial assets. This can widen the gap between the wealthy and the poor, as those without significant assets do not benefit as directly from rising asset prices.

3. Independence of Central Banks:

- The independence of central banks is crucial to maintaining a balanced approach to money creation. Political interference in monetary policy can lead to irresponsible money creation, driven by short-term political goals rather than long-term economic stability. Independent central banks can make decisions based on economic data and principles, reducing the risk of inflation and financial instability.

Modern Innovations in Money Creation

1. Digital Currencies:

- The rise of digital currencies, including cryptocurrencies and central bank digital currencies (CBDCs), is transforming the landscape of money creation. Cryptocurrencies like Bitcoin are created through decentralized networks and mining processes, challenging traditional notions of money creation and control.

- CBDCs represent a new form of digital money issued by central banks, combining the benefits of digital transactions with the stability of traditional currency. These innovations could enhance financial inclusion, reduce transaction costs, and improve the efficiency of monetary policy.

2. Financial Technology (Fintech):

- Fintech innovations are revolutionizing how money is created, distributed, and managed. Peer-to-peer lending, crowdfunding platforms, and digital payment systems are expanding access to financial services and enabling new forms of money creation outside traditional banking systems.

The Future of Money Creation

1. Sustainable Money Creation:

- Future approaches to money creation will likely emphasize sustainability and resilience. Balancing economic growth with environmental and social considerations will be key to ensuring that money creation supports long-term prosperity without causing harm.

2. Global Coordination:

- As economies become increasingly interconnected, global coordination in monetary policy will become more important. International organizations like the International Monetary Fund (IMF) and the Bank for International Settlements (BIS) play a crucial role in fostering cooperation and stability in global money-creation practices.

Conclusion: Harnessing the Power of Money Creation

The power of money creation is immense, with profound implications for economic growth, stability, and equity. Understanding the mechanisms and impacts of money creation is essential for policymakers, businesses, and individuals alike. By harnessing this power responsibly and innovatively, we can build a financial system that promotes sustainable and inclusive economic progress.

As we conclude this exploration of money and its myriad facets, we are reminded of the importance of vigilance, innovation, and cooperation in shaping a future where the benefits of money creation are shared equitably, and the risks are carefully managed.

CHAPTER 04

THE POWER OF MONEY TO CREATE INEQUALITY AND WEALTH

The Dual Nature of Money

Money is a powerful force with the capacity to generate both immense wealth and significant inequality. While it can drive economic growth and prosperity, it can also lead to vast disparities in wealth distribution. Understanding how money contributes to both wealth creation and inequality is crucial for addressing the challenges of modern economies and fostering a more equitable society.

Wealth Creation: The Positive Side of Money

1. Entrepreneurship and Innovation:

- Money fuels entrepreneurship and innovation, enabling individuals to start and grow businesses. Access to capital allows entrepreneurs to develop new products, enter markets, and create jobs. Successful ventures generate wealth for business owners, employees, and investors, contributing to economic growth and societal progress.

2. Investment and Economic Growth:

- Investments in infrastructure, technology, and education drive economic development. Public and private investments improve productivity, enhance living standards, and create new opportunities for wealth generation. Financial markets provide a platform for individuals and institutions to invest in promising ventures, spreading wealth across the economy.

3. Access to Opportunities:

- Financial resources provide access to opportunities that can significantly enhance one's economic position. Education, healthcare, and professional development often require substantial financial investment. Those with access to money can afford better education and healthcare, positioning themselves and their descendants for long-term success.

Inequality: The Negative Side of Money

1. Unequal Access to Capital:

- One of the primary drivers of inequality is the unequal access to capital. Individuals and communities with limited financial resources struggle to invest in opportunities that could improve their economic status. This disparity creates a cycle of poverty, where those without money remain economically disadvantaged.

2. Wealth Concentration:

- The concentration of wealth in the hands of a few exacerbates inequality. Wealthy individuals and families often have access to exclusive investment opportunities, generating returns that further increase their wealth. This concentration of wealth can lead to economic and political power imbalances, where the wealthy have disproportionate influence over policies and decisions.

3. Wage Disparities:

- Significant disparities in wages and salaries contribute to economic inequality. High-income individuals, particularly in finance, technology, and executive roles, earn substantially more than those in lower-paying jobs. This wage gap limits upward mobility and perpetuates economic divides.

Mechanisms of Wealth Creation and Inequality

1. Financial Markets and Investment:

- Financial markets play a crucial role in wealth creation but can also widen the gap between rich and poor. Stock ownership, for instance, is heavily skewed toward the wealthy. While the stock market provides substantial returns over time, those without the means to invest miss out on these gains, exacerbating wealth inequality.

2. Real Estate:

- Real estate is another significant avenue for wealth creation. Property ownership can provide rental income, tax benefits, and long-term appreciation. However, rising property prices can also lead to housing affordability issues, particularly in urban areas, creating a barrier to homeownership for lower-income individuals.

3. Inheritance and Intergenerational Wealth:

- Wealth is often passed down through generations, creating enduring economic advantages for certain families. Inherited wealth can include financial assets, real estate, and business interests, providing a substantial head start for future generations. This intergenerational transfer of wealth perpetuates inequality.

4. Education and Skill Development:

- Access to quality education and skill development is closely linked to economic mobility. Those with financial resources can afford better education, leading to higher-paying jobs and more significant career opportunities. Conversely, lack of access to quality education can trap individuals in low-wage jobs, limiting their economic prospects.

Addressing Wealth Inequality

1. Progressive Taxation:

- Progressive taxation, where higher income earners pay a larger percentage of their income in taxes, can help redistribute wealth and fund social programs. Effective tax policies can reduce income inequality and provide resources for public services that benefit lower-income individuals.

2. Access to Education and Training:

- Ensuring equitable access to quality education and vocational training is essential for reducing inequality. Public investment in education, scholarships, and affordable training programs can help level the playing field and provide opportunities for economic advancement.

3. Social Safety Nets:

- Robust social safety nets, including unemployment benefits, healthcare, and housing assistance, can protect vulnerable populations from economic shocks. These programs provide a buffer against poverty and help individuals and families maintain stability during difficult times.

4. Financial Inclusion:

- Promoting financial inclusion by providing access to banking, credit, and investment opportunities for underserved communities can help reduce inequality. Microfinance, mobile banking, and community investment initiatives can empower individuals to build wealth and improve their economic status.

5. Corporate Responsibility:

- Corporations have a role to play in addressing inequality. Fair wages, ethical business practices, and community engagement can contribute to a more equitable distribution of wealth. Companies that prioritize social and environmental responsibility can positively impact society and reduce economic disparities.

Conclusion: Balancing Wealth and Inequality

Money has the power to create both wealth and inequality. While it can drive economic growth and provide opportunities for financial success, it can also perpetuate disparities and limit upward mobility. Addressing the complex interplay between wealth creation and inequality requires comprehensive strategies that promote equitable access to opportunities, fair distribution of resources, and responsible economic policies.

As we navigate the future of finance, it is essential to recognize the dual nature of money and work towards a system that fosters both prosperity and fairness. By embracing inclusive and sustainable practices, we can harness the power of money to build a more equitable and thriving society for all.

CHAPTER 05

THE POWER OF MONEY TO WREAK DEVASTATION

The Destructive Potential of Money

While money can be a force for good, driving economic growth and improving living standards, it also has the potential to cause significant devastation. From financial crises to environmental destruction, the misuse and mismanagement of money can lead to far-reaching negative consequences. This chapter explores how money can wreak devastation, examining historical examples and the underlying mechanisms that contribute to such outcomes.

Financial Crises: The Ripple Effects of Economic Collapse

1. The Great Depression:

- The Great Depression of the 1930s serves as a stark reminder of how financial instability can lead to widespread economic devastation. Triggered by the stock market crash of 1929, the depression resulted in massive unemployment, bank failures, and severe economic contraction. The misallocation of capital, speculative bubbles, and inadequate regulatory frameworks were significant contributors to this crisis.

2. The 2008 Financial Crisis:

- The 2008 financial crisis, sparked by the collapse of the housing market and the failure of major financial institutions, had global repercussions. Excessive risk-taking, complex financial instruments, and insufficient oversight led to the crisis, resulting in trillions of dollars in losses, widespread foreclosures, and long-lasting economic repercussions.

3. Currency Crises:

- Currency crises, such as the 1997 Asian Financial Crisis, demonstrate how rapid capital flight and currency devaluation can destabilize entire economies. These crises often lead to severe recessions, high inflation, and increased poverty, with devastating impacts on affected populations.

Environmental Destruction: The Cost of Unchecked Growth

1. Industrial Pollution:

   - The relentless pursuit of economic growth often comes at the expense of the environment. Industrial activities release pollutants into the air, water, and soil, causing significant harm to ecosystems and human health. For instance, the smog and air pollution in cities like Beijing and Delhi have reached critical levels, impacting millions of residents.

2. Deforestation and Habitat Loss:

   - Economic activities, such as logging, mining, and agriculture, drive deforestation and habitat loss. The Amazon rainforest, often referred to as the "lungs of the Earth," has seen extensive deforestation due to these activities, threatening biodiversity and contributing to climate change.

3. Climate Change:

   - The burning of fossil fuels for energy and transportation is a significant contributor to climate change. Rising global temperatures, melting ice caps, and increasing frequency of extreme weather events are all consequences of unchecked carbon emissions. The economic costs of climate change, including damage to infrastructure, loss of agricultural productivity, and health impacts, are immense.

Social Unrest and Inequality: The Human Toll

1. Income Inequality:

- The concentration of wealth in the hands of a few exacerbates social inequalities and fuels social unrest. Economic policies that favor the wealthy, such as tax cuts for high-income earners and deregulation of financial markets, can widen the gap between rich and poor. This disparity often leads to political instability and social tensions.

2. Exploitation and Labor Issues:

- The drive for profit can result in the exploitation of workers, particularly in developing countries. Sweatshops, child labor, and unsafe working conditions are byproducts of cost-cutting measures by corporations seeking to maximize profits. These practices not only harm workers but also undermine human rights and dignity.

3. Displacement and Migration:

- Economic projects, such as large-scale infrastructure developments and resource extraction, can displace communities and disrupt traditional ways of life. Forced evictions and land grabs leave people without homes or livelihoods, contributing to migration and social dislocation.

Corruption and Governance: The Erosion of Trust

1. Political Corruption:

- The misuse of public funds and bribery erode trust in government institutions and hinder economic development. Corruption diverts resources from essential public services, such as healthcare and education, and undermines the rule of law. Countries with high levels of corruption often face chronic poverty and instability.

2. Corporate Malfeasance:

- Corporate scandals, such as accounting fraud and insider trading, can devastate investors and employees. Companies like Enron and WorldCom engaged in fraudulent practices that ultimately led to their collapse, erasing billions in shareholder value and causing significant job losses.

3. Financial Mismanagement:

- Poor financial management at both the corporate and governmental levels can lead to severe economic consequences. Misallocation of resources, excessive borrowing, and fiscal irresponsibility can result in debt crises and economic downturns, impacting millions of people.

Preventing Devastation: Towards Responsible Financial Practices

1. Regulatory Reforms:

   - Strengthening regulatory frameworks and oversight can mitigate the risks of financial crises and corporate malfeasance. Transparent and accountable governance, combined with effective enforcement mechanisms, can prevent the misuse of money and protect the public interest.

2. Sustainable Development:

   - Embracing sustainable development practices can balance economic growth with environmental preservation. Investing in renewable energy, promoting resource efficiency, and protecting natural habitats are essential steps towards a more sustainable future.

3. Social Equity:

   - Addressing social inequalities through progressive taxation, fair wages, and social safety nets can reduce the human toll of economic activities. Policies that promote inclusive growth and equitable distribution of resources are vital for fostering social cohesion and stability.

4. Ethical Business Practices:

- Corporations must adopt ethical business practices that prioritize long-term value over short-term profits. Corporate social responsibility, environmental stewardship, and fair labor practices are crucial for building trust and ensuring sustainable business operations.

Conclusion: Harnessing the Power of Money Responsibly

The power of money to wreak devastation is undeniable, but so is its potential to drive positive change. By recognizing the destructive capabilities of money and implementing responsible financial practices, we can mitigate the negative impacts and create a more equitable and sustainable future. Understanding the dual nature of money is essential for navigating the complexities of modern economies and ensuring that the benefits of economic growth are shared widely and fairly.

CHAPTER 06

THE POWER OF INTERNATIONAL MONEY

The Global Influence of Capital Flows

International money, encompassing foreign investment, trade, and financial aid, plays a critical role in shaping the economic landscape of nations. The movement of capital across borders has profound implications for development, stability, and international relations. This chapter explores the power of international money, its mechanisms, and its impacts on the global economy.

Foreign Direct Investment (FDI): A Catalyst for Growth

1. Economic Development:

   - Foreign direct investment involves multinational companies investing in production, infrastructure, or other business activities in another country. FDI can spur economic growth by creating jobs, transferring technology, and enhancing productivity. For example, the influx of FDI into China over the past few decades has significantly contributed to its rapid economic growth and modernization.

2. Market Access and Integration:

- FDI provides host countries with access to new markets and integration into global supply chains. This integration can enhance competitiveness and foster economic diversification. Countries like Vietnam have benefited from FDI by becoming key players in global manufacturing networks.

3. Challenges and Risks:

- While FDI can bring substantial benefits, it also poses challenges. Dependence on foreign capital can lead to economic vulnerability, and the repatriation of profits by multinational companies can limit the long-term benefits for the host country. Moreover, FDI can sometimes lead to the exploitation of local resources and labor.

International Trade: The Lifeblood of Globalization

1. Trade Agreements and Economic Growth:

- International trade agreements, such as the North American Free Trade Agreement (NAFTA) and the

European Union (EU) single market, facilitate the free flow of goods and services across borders. These agreements can boost economic growth by expanding markets, reducing tariffs, and encouraging competition.

2. Comparative Advantage:

- Trade allows countries to specialize in producing goods and services in which they have a comparative advantage, leading to more efficient resource allocation and increased productivity. For instance, Japan's specialization in technology and automotive industries has been a key driver of its economic success.

3. Trade Imbalances:

- Persistent trade imbalances, where a country imports more than it exports, can lead to economic instability and tensions. The trade deficit between the United States and China has been a source of economic and political friction, highlighting the complexities of international trade relationships.

International Aid and Development Assistance:

1. Humanitarian Aid:

- International aid, including humanitarian assistance, plays a crucial role in addressing immediate needs during crises such as natural disasters, conflicts, and pandemics. Organizations like the United Nations and various non-governmental organizations (NGOs) provide vital support to affected populations, helping to alleviate suffering and stabilize regions.

2. Development Aid:

   - Long-term development aid aims to promote economic development and improve living standards in developing countries. This aid can fund infrastructure projects, education, healthcare, and capacity-building initiatives. Countries like South Korea have transitioned from aid recipients to developed economies, demonstrating the potential impact of sustained development assistance.

3. Aid Effectiveness:

   - The effectiveness of international aid is often debated. Critics argue that aid can create dependency, encourage corruption, and fail to reach those in need. However, proponents highlight successes in reducing poverty, improving health outcomes, and supporting sustainable development. Ensuring transparency, accountability, and local involvement is essential for maximizing the impact of aid.

Global Financial Markets: The Engines of Capital Flow

1. Foreign Exchange Markets:

- The foreign exchange (forex) market is the largest financial market globally, where currencies are traded. Exchange rates impact international trade, investment, and economic stability. Volatility in forex markets can lead to significant economic consequences, influencing inflation, export competitiveness, and capital flows.

2. Sovereign Debt:

- Countries borrow from international markets to finance development projects and manage economic cycles. Sovereign debt markets provide access to capital but also expose countries to risks of debt crises. The European sovereign debt crisis highlighted the vulnerabilities of high debt levels and the interconnectedness of global financial systems.

3. Financial Crises and Contagion:

- Global financial markets can transmit economic shocks across borders, leading to crises. The 2008 financial crisis, which began in the United States, quickly spread worldwide, demonstrating the interconnected nature of modern financial systems. Coordinated international responses, such as those led by the International Monetary

Fund (IMF), are often required to stabilize affected economies.

Remittances: Lifelines for Developing Economies

1. Economic Impact:

- Remittances, the money sent home by migrant workers, are a significant source of income for many developing countries. These funds support household consumption, education, healthcare, and small businesses. Countries like India, Mexico, and the Philippines receive substantial remittance inflows, which bolster their economies.

2. Financial Inclusion:

- Remittances can enhance financial inclusion by encouraging the use of formal financial services, such as bank accounts and mobile money platforms. Access to these services helps recipients save, invest, and improve their financial resilience.

3. Challenges:

- High transaction costs and limited access to formal financial channels can reduce the effectiveness of remittances. Efforts to reduce fees and expand financial access are crucial for maximizing the benefits of these flows.

The Role of International Institutions:

1. International Monetary Fund (IMF):

- The IMF provides financial assistance and policy advice to countries facing economic instability. It plays a critical role in stabilizing economies, supporting structural reforms, and promoting global economic cooperation. However, IMF programs are sometimes criticized for imposing austerity measures that can exacerbate social hardships.

2. World Bank:
- The World Bank focuses on long-term development projects and poverty reduction. It provides financing, expertise, and technical assistance to developing countries. The Bank's initiatives in infrastructure, education, and health have contributed to significant development progress, but it faces challenges in addressing complex and evolving global needs.

3. World Trade Organization (WTO):
- The WTO regulates international trade and resolves trade disputes among member countries. It aims to promote free and fair trade, contributing to global economic growth. The organization's effectiveness is often debated, particularly regarding its ability to address modern trade challenges and protect the interests of developing nations.

Conclusion: The Transformative Power of International Money

International money, through mechanisms like FDI, trade, aid, and remittances, wields significant power to influence global economic dynamics. While it can drive development and foster international cooperation, it also poses challenges and risks that require careful management and coordination. Understanding the multifaceted impacts of international money is essential for policymakers, businesses, and individuals navigating the complexities of the global economy.

As we move forward, fostering a balanced and equitable approach to international capital flows will be crucial for ensuring that the benefits of globalization are shared widely and sustainably. By addressing the challenges and leveraging the opportunities presented by international money, we can build a more prosperous and interconnected world.

CHAPTER 07

THE ECONOMIC ENGINE

The Heartbeat of Economies

Money serves as the lifeblood of economies, driving transactions, investments, and growth. Its role in the economic engine is multifaceted, encompassing concepts like supply and demand, inflation, and the global financial systems that interconnect nations. Understanding these elements is crucial to comprehending how economies function and thrive.

The Basics of Supply and Demand

At the core of any economy is the principle of supply and demand. This fundamental concept dictates the price and quantity of goods and services in a market. When demand exceeds supply, prices rise, encouraging producers to increase production. Conversely, when supply surpasses demand, prices fall, prompting consumers to buy more.

Money as a Medium of Exchange

Money simplifies the process of exchange by acting as a universally accepted medium. It eliminates the inefficiencies of barter systems, enabling people to trade goods and services with ease. This efficiency drives economic activity, allowing markets to grow and diversify.

The Role of Banks and Financial Institutions

Banks and financial institutions play a critical role in the economic engine by managing the flow of money. They provide essential services like savings accounts, loans, and investments, which facilitate business operations and personal financial planning. By offering credit, banks help businesses expand and innovate, driving economic growth.

Inflation: The Double-Edged Sword

Inflation, the rate at which the general level of prices for goods and services rises, erodes purchasing power over time. Moderate inflation is a sign of a growing economy, as it encourages spending and investment. However, hyperinflation can destabilize economies, leading to uncertainty and reduced economic activity. Central banks, like the Federal Reserve in the United States, aim to manage inflation through monetary policy.

Monetary Policy and Economic Stability

Monetary policy involves regulating the money supply and interest rates to influence economic activity. Central banks use tools like open market operations, discount rates, and reserve requirements to control inflation and stabilize the economy. By adjusting interest rates, central banks can either encourage borrowing and spending (lower rates) or curb inflation and overheating (higher rates).

The Global Financial System

The global financial system is an intricate web of interconnected markets and institutions. It facilitates international trade, investment, and the movement of capital across borders. Key components include foreign exchange markets, international banks, and supranational institutions like the International Monetary Fund (IMF) and the World Bank.

Exchange Rates and International Trade

Exchange rates, the value of one currency relative to another, play a crucial role in international trade. They affect the competitiveness of a country's goods and services in the global market. A strong currency makes exports more expensive and imports cheaper, while a weak currency has the opposite effect. Governments and central banks may intervene in currency markets to stabilize or manipulate exchange rates for economic advantage.

Financial Markets and Investment

Financial markets, including stock exchanges, bond markets, and commodity markets, provide platforms for buying and selling financial assets. These markets are vital for raising capital, distributing risk, and signaling economic trends. Investors, ranging from individuals to large institutions, participate in these markets to grow wealth and diversify portfolios.

Economic Indicators and Their Impact

Economic indicators, such as Gross Domestic Product (GDP), unemployment rates, and consumer confidence indices, provide insights into the health of an economy. Policymakers, investors, and businesses use these indicators to make informed decisions. For instance, a rising GDP indicates economic growth, while high unemployment may signal economic distress.

Challenges and Opportunities in the Modern Economy

The modern economy faces numerous challenges and opportunities, from technological advancements to environmental concerns. Innovations like blockchain and cryptocurrencies are reshaping financial systems, while climate change prompts a shift towards sustainable economic practices. Navigating these changes requires adaptability and forward-thinking strategies.

Conclusion: The Dynamic Economic Engine

Money drives the economic engine, powering transactions, investments, and growth. Its role in supply and demand, inflation management, and the global financial system underscores its importance in maintaining economic stability and prosperity. By understanding these concepts, we gain a clearer picture of how economies function and the factors that influence their success.

In the next chapter, we will explore the darker side of money, examining ethical dilemmas and the negative consequences associated with the pursuit of wealth.

CHAPTER 08

THE PURSUIT OF WEALTH AND ITS SHADOWS

While money drives economic growth and prosperity, it also casts a long shadow, revealing the darker side of human ambition. The pursuit of wealth can lead to ethical dilemmas and negative consequences, ranging from corruption and inequality to environmental degradation. Understanding these issues is crucial to fostering a more equitable and sustainable economic system.

Corruption: The Moral Decay

Corruption is one of the most pervasive negative consequences associated with the pursuit of wealth. It manifests in various forms, including bribery, embezzlement, and fraud. Corruption undermines trust in institutions, distorts markets, and diverts resources from essential public services. Countries with high levels of corruption often experience slower economic growth, increased inequality, and social unrest.

Economic Inequality: The Wealth Gap

The concentration of wealth in the hands of a few leads to significant economic inequality. This wealth gap creates social and economic divides, limiting opportunities for the less fortunate. Inequality can result in reduced social mobility, where individuals find it challenging to improve their economic status regardless of their talents or efforts. Addressing this issue requires policies that promote fair wages, access to education, and social safety nets.

Exploitation and Labor Issues

In the relentless pursuit of profit, businesses sometimes exploit workers, leading to poor working conditions, low wages, and inadequate benefits. Child labor and modern slavery are extreme examples of such exploitation. Ethical business practices and stronger labor regulations are necessary to protect workers' rights and ensure fair treatment in the workplace.

Environmental Degradation: The Cost of Growth

The quest for economic growth often comes at the expense of the environment. Industrial activities, deforestation, and overexploitation of natural resources lead to environmental degradation, climate change, and loss of biodiversity. The long-term consequences of these actions threaten the planet's health and the well-being of future generations. Sustainable practices and policies are crucial to mitigating these effects and promoting environmental stewardship.

Financial Crises: The Boom and Bust Cycles

The financial system is prone to cycles of boom and bust, where periods of rapid economic growth are followed by severe downturns. These cycles are often fueled by excessive risk-taking, speculative investments, and inadequate regulation. Financial crises, such as the Great Depression and the 2008 financial crisis, have devastating effects on economies, leading to massive job losses, reduced wealth, and long-term economic stagnation.

Consumerism: The Culture of Excess

Consumerism, driven by the desire for material possessions, contributes to environmental degradation and social inequalities. The culture of excess promotes unsustainable consumption patterns, leading to overproduction, waste, and resource depletion. Shifting towards a more mindful and sustainable consumption model can help address these issues and reduce the negative impact on the environment and society.

Corporate Power and Influence

Large corporations wield significant power and influence over political and economic systems. This influence can lead to regulatory capture, where industries manipulate regulations to their advantage, often at the expense of the public interest. Corporate lobbying and political donations can also skew policy decisions, undermining democratic processes and perpetuating inequality.

Tax Evasion and Avoidance

Tax evasion and avoidance by wealthy individuals and corporations deprive governments of crucial revenue needed for public services and infrastructure. These practices exacerbate inequality and place a disproportionate tax burden on ordinary citizens. Strengthening tax laws and closing loopholes are essential steps in ensuring a fairer tax system and reducing inequality.

Cultural and Social Impacts

The relentless pursuit of wealth can erode cultural values and social cohesion. Materialism can overshadow community values, leading to increased stress, mental health issues, and weakened social bonds. Promoting a balanced approach to wealth, where personal well-being and community welfare are prioritized, can help mitigate these negative cultural and social impacts.

Conclusion: Navigating the Dark Side

The dark side of dollars highlights the ethical dilemmas and negative consequences associated with the pursuit of wealth. Addressing these issues requires a multi-faceted approach, involving stronger regulations, ethical business practices, sustainable policies, and a cultural shift towards more mindful consumption. By acknowledging and addressing the dark side of money, we can work towards a more just, equitable, and sustainable economic system.

In the next chapter, we will explore the various strategies people employ to amass wealth, including investments, entrepreneurship, and the impact of technological advancements.

CHAPTER 09

THE PATHWAYS TO WEALTH

Accumulating wealth is an art that involves a combination of strategies, insights, and often a bit of luck. From traditional investments to modern technological advancements, individuals have various avenues to build and grow their financial assets. This chapter explores these pathways, highlighting the key strategies and principles that can lead to substantial wealth accumulation.

Investments: The Foundation of Wealth

Investing is one of the most common and effective ways to accumulate wealth. By putting money into assets that have the potential to grow over time, individuals can increase their wealth significantly. Key investment strategies include:

1. Stock Market Investing:

   - Equities: Investing in stocks represents ownership in a company and entitles the investor to a share of the profits. Historically, the stock market has offered high returns, but it also comes with risks.

   - Bonds: Bonds are debt securities issued by governments or corporations. They provide regular interest payments and are generally considered safer than stocks but offer lower returns.

2. Real Estate:

   - Real estate investments involve purchasing properties to generate rental income or to sell at a higher price. Real estate can be a stable investment, offering both capital appreciation and cash flow.

3. Mutual Funds and ETFs:

   - These investment vehicles pool money from multiple investors to buy a diversified portfolio of stocks, bonds, or other assets. They offer diversification and professional management, making them accessible to average investors.

4. Commodities:

- Investing in physical commodities like gold, silver, oil, and agricultural products can be a hedge against inflation and market volatility.

Entrepreneurship: Creating Wealth from Scratch

Entrepreneurship is a powerful engine for wealth creation. By starting and growing businesses, entrepreneurs can generate substantial wealth and create value for society. Key aspects of successful entrepreneurship include:

1. Innovation:

- Developing new products, services, or business models that meet market needs can lead to significant financial rewards.

2. Risk Management:

- Entrepreneurs must be willing to take calculated risks and manage uncertainties effectively. This involves thorough market research, strategic planning, and adaptable business practices.

3. Scaling Up:

- Successful businesses often grow by scaling their operations, expanding their market reach, and increasing their customer base. This can involve securing funding, hiring talent, and improving operational efficiencies.

4. Exit Strategies:

- Entrepreneurs can accumulate wealth by selling their businesses through mergers, acquisitions, or initial public offerings (IPOs). These exits can provide substantial financial returns.

The Impact of Technological Advancements

Technology has revolutionized the way people accumulate wealth. Innovations in finance, information technology, and automation have created new opportunities and transformed traditional industries. Key technological impacts include:

1. Fintech:

- Financial technology (fintech) has democratized access to financial services, allowing individuals to invest, save, and borrow more efficiently. Platforms like robo-advisors, peer-to-peer lending, and blockchain technology have opened up new avenues for wealth accumulation.

2. E-commerce:

- The rise of online retail has enabled entrepreneurs to reach global markets with minimal upfront costs. E-commerce platforms like Amazon, eBay, and Shopify have empowered small businesses and individual sellers.

3. Automation and AI:

- Automation and artificial intelligence (AI) are reshaping industries by increasing productivity and reducing costs. These technologies create opportunities for new business ventures and investment strategies.

4. Cryptocurrencies:

- Cryptocurrencies, like Bitcoin and Ethereum, have emerged as alternative investment assets. While highly volatile, they offer the potential for significant returns and have attracted considerable interest from investors.

Wealth Management: Protecting and Growing Assets

Accumulating wealth is only part of the equation; managing and protecting it is equally important. Effective wealth management involves:

1. Diversification:

- Spreading investments across various asset classes and sectors to reduce risk.

2. Tax Planning:

- Implementing strategies to minimize tax liabilities and maximize after-tax returns.

3. Estate Planning:

- Ensuring that wealth is preserved and transferred according to the individual's wishes through wills, trusts, and other legal instruments.

4. Financial Advising:

- Consulting with financial advisors to develop comprehensive wealth management plans that align with personal goals and risk tolerance.

Conclusion: Mastering the Art of Wealth Accumulation

The art of accumulating wealth involves a blend of strategic investments, entrepreneurial ventures, and leveraging technological advancements. By understanding and applying these strategies, individuals can effectively grow their financial assets and achieve long-term financial success. In the next chapter, we will investigate the close relationship between money and political influence, exploring historical and contemporary examples of how wealth shapes governance.

CHAPTER 10

MONEY AND POWER

The Interplay of Wealth and Governance

Money and power are intrinsically linked, with wealth often serving as a means to attain and exert political influence. Throughout history, those with financial resources have shaped governance structures, influenced policy decisions, and directed the course of nations. This chapter explores the dynamic relationship between money and power, highlighting key historical and contemporary examples.

Historical Foundations of Wealth and Power

1. The Medici Family:

- In Renaissance Italy, the Medici family used their banking fortune to gain political control of Florence. Their wealth allowed them to sponsor art, influence church appointments, and manipulate political outcomes. The Medici's patronage of the arts and sciences left a lasting cultural legacy, but their political machinations also demonstrated the extent to which money could buy power.

2. The East India Company:

- The British East India Company, a powerful trading corporation, played a pivotal role in British colonial expansion. With its own private army and significant financial resources, the company exerted substantial influence over British foreign policy and governance in India. This blend of corporate and political power had far-reaching consequences for both the colonizers and the colonized.

The Role of Money in Modern Politics

1. Campaign Financing:

- In contemporary democracies, political campaigns require significant funding. Wealthy individuals and corporations often contribute large sums to candidates and parties that align with their interests. This financial support can translate into political favors, policy influence, and regulatory advantages. The debate over campaign finance reform highlights the tension between free speech and the risk of undue influence.

2. Lobbying:

- Lobbying is a multi-billion dollar industry where interest groups, corporations, and advocacy organizations seek to influence legislators and government officials. Lobbyists use financial contributions, strategic communication, and personal relationships to shape policy decisions. While lobbying can provide valuable insights to policymakers, it also raises concerns about unequal access and the potential for corruption.

3. The Revolving Door:

- The "revolving door" phenomenon refers to the movement of individuals between roles in government and positions in the private sector. Former politicians and regulators often join corporations as executives or consultants, leveraging their insider knowledge and connections. This practice can create conflicts of interest and raise questions about the integrity of public decision-making.

Wealth and Political Power in Authoritarian Regimes

1. Oligarchies:

- In some countries, a small group of wealthy individuals, or oligarchs, wield significant political power. Russia, for example, has seen the rise of oligarchs who control vast sectors of the economy and exert considerable influence over government policies. These oligarchs often benefit from close relationships with political leaders, reinforcing a cycle of mutual support and control.

2. State Capitalism:

- In state capitalist systems, governments exert control over key industries and use economic power to maintain political authority. China exemplifies this model, where state-owned enterprises play a crucial role in the economy, and the government uses financial resources to promote national interests and sustain its rule.

Money, Power, and Social Inequality

1. Influence on Legislation:

- Wealthy individuals and interest groups can influence legislation in ways that benefit their economic interests, often at the expense of broader social equity. For example, tax policies, labor laws, and regulatory frameworks can be shaped to favor the rich, exacerbating income inequality and limiting social mobility.

2. Access to Justice:

- Money can also affect access to justice. Wealthy individuals and corporations can afford top legal representation, potentially skewing legal outcomes in their favor. This disparity undermines the principle of equal justice under the law and can erode public trust in legal institutions.

Case Studies: Money and Power in Action

1. The Koch Brothers:

- Charles and David Koch, billionaire industrialists, have used their wealth to influence American politics through extensive funding of conservative causes, think tanks, and political candidates. Their financial contributions have shaped debates on climate change, healthcare, and regulatory policies.

2. Silicon Valley and Political Influence:

- Technology giants like Google, Facebook, and Amazon have increasingly flexed their financial muscles in the political arena. Through lobbying efforts, campaign donations, and strategic partnerships, these companies seek to influence policies on data privacy, antitrust regulations, and digital economy issues.

Conclusion: Navigating the Nexus of Money and Power

The close relationship between money and political influence underscores the complex interplay between economic resources and governance. While wealth can drive progress and innovation, it can also lead to unequal access and potential corruption. Addressing these challenges requires transparency, accountability, and robust legal frameworks to ensure that political power serves the broader public interest.

In the next chapter, we will discuss the geopolitical implications of currency manipulation, trade wars, and the power struggles that arise from economic competition on a global scale.

CHAPTER 11

THE BATTLEFIELDS OF GLOBAL FINANCE

Currency wars, also known as competitive devaluations, occur when countries intentionally devalue their currencies to gain a trade advantage. This practice, along with trade wars and economic competition, shapes the geopolitical landscape, influencing global power dynamics and economic stability. This chapter explores the implications of these economic strategies and the power struggles they generate on a global scale.

The Mechanics of Currency Manipulation

1. Devaluation and Trade Balance:

- Currency devaluation makes a country's exports cheaper and imports more expensive, boosting export competitiveness and reducing trade deficits. This strategy can stimulate domestic industries but often leads to retaliation from trading partners.

2. Monetary Policy and Exchange Rates:

- Central banks play a crucial role in currency manipulation through monetary policy. By adjusting interest rates and engaging in open market operations, central banks can influence the value of their currency. For example, lowering interest rates can devalue a currency by making it less attractive to foreign investors.

Historical Examples of Currency Wars

1. The Great Depression:

- During the Great Depression, countries like the United States, the United Kingdom, and France engaged in competitive devaluations to boost their economies. This "beggar-thy-neighbor" policy led to a spiral of retaliatory actions, exacerbating global economic instability.

2. The Plaza Accord:

- In 1985, the United States, Japan, West Germany, France, and the United Kingdom agreed to the Plaza Accord, which aimed to depreciate the US dollar relative to the Japanese yen and German mark. This agreement temporarily stabilized exchange rates and addressed trade imbalances.

The Geopolitical Implications of Currency Manipulation

1. Trade Wars:

- Currency manipulation often triggers trade wars, where countries impose tariffs, quotas, and other barriers to protect their domestic industries. These actions can escalate into broader economic conflicts, disrupting global supply chains and increasing tensions between nations.

2. Economic Sanctions:

- Countries may use economic sanctions as a tool to exert political pressure or punish adversaries. Sanctions can include restrictions on trade, financial transactions, and access to international markets, severely impacting the targeted economy.

3. Shifting Alliances:

- Currency manipulation and trade policies can lead to shifts in global alliances. Countries may seek new trade partners or strengthen existing relationships to counterbalance economic pressures. These realignments can alter geopolitical landscapes and influence global power structures.

Case Study: US-China Trade and Currency Conflict

1. The Yuan-Dollar Dynamic:

- The United States has accused China of deliberately devaluing its currency, the yuan, to gain a trade advantage. China's exchange rate policies have been a focal point of trade tensions between the two economic giants.

2. Tariffs and Trade Barriers:

- The US-China trade war, marked by tit-for-tat tariffs and trade barriers, has disrupted global markets and supply chains. Both countries have sought to protect their domestic industries while exerting pressure on each other's economies.

3. Geopolitical Ramifications:

- The US-China economic conflict has broader geopolitical implications, influencing global alliances, regional stability, and international institutions. The trade war has also accelerated the decoupling of the two economies, prompting shifts in global trade patterns.

Currency Wars in Emerging Markets

1. Vulnerability to External Shocks:

- Emerging markets are particularly vulnerable to currency wars and global economic competition. Rapid currency devaluations can lead to inflation, capital flight, and economic instability.

2. Defensive Measures:

- To protect their economies, emerging markets may implement capital controls, seek financial assistance from international institutions, or engage in currency interventions to stabilize their exchange rates.

The Role of International Institutions

1. The International Monetary Fund (IMF):

- The IMF monitors global economic stability and provides financial assistance to countries facing currency crises. It also offers policy advice and support to help nations navigate the complexities of global economic competition.

2. The World Trade Organization (WTO):

- The WTO mediates trade disputes and sets rules for international trade. Its role in resolving conflicts and promoting fair trade practices is crucial in mitigating the impacts of trade wars and currency manipulation.

Conclusion: Navigating the Complexities of Currency Wars

Currency wars and trade conflicts are central to the geopolitical power struggles of the modern world. Understanding the mechanics of currency manipulation and its far-reaching implications is essential for navigating these complex dynamics. By fostering international cooperation and adhering to fair economic practices, nations can mitigate the negative impacts of these conflicts and promote global economic stability.

In the next chapter, we will highlight stories of individuals who overcame adversity to achieve financial success, showcasing the diverse paths people take to accumulate wealth.

CHAPTER 12

FROM RAGS TO RICHES

The Journey of Transformation

The journey from rags to riches is a powerful testament to human resilience, determination, and ingenuity. Throughout history, individuals have overcome immense adversity to achieve remarkable financial success. This chapter highlights inspiring stories of people who defied the odds, showcasing the diverse paths they took to accumulate wealth and the lessons we can learn from their experiences.

1. Andrew Carnegie: The Steel Tycoon

Background:

- Born in 1835 in Dunfermline, Scotland, Andrew Carnegie grew up in a poor family that immigrated to the

United States in search of a better life. Starting as a bobbin boy in a cotton factory, Carnegie worked tirelessly to improve his circumstances.

Path to Wealth:

- Carnegie's journey to wealth began with a series of smart investments in the railroad and steel industries. He founded the Carnegie Steel Company, which became the largest and most profitable steel company in the world.

Legacy:

- Carnegie became one of the richest men in history and was a prominent philanthropist, donating much of his fortune to educational and cultural institutions. His life exemplifies the power of perseverance and strategic investment.

2. Oprah Winfrey: The Media Mogul

Background:

- Oprah Winfrey was born in 1954 in rural Mississippi to a single teenage mother. She faced numerous challenges, including poverty, abuse, and discrimination, but her determination to succeed was unwavering.

Path to Wealth:

- Winfrey's career in media began with a job in radio, eventually leading to her breakthrough as the host of "The

Oprah Winfrey Show." Her charisma and authenticity resonated with audiences, propelling her to become a media mogul with her own production company, Harpo Productions.

Legacy:

- Winfrey's influence extends beyond media; she is a philanthropist, author, and advocate for various social causes. Her story highlights the importance of self-belief, hard work, and leveraging one's unique talents.

3. Howard Schultz: The Starbucks Visionary

Background:

- Howard Schultz was born in 1953 in Brooklyn, New York, to a poor family. He experienced financial hardships growing up, which fueled his ambition to create a better life.

Path to Wealth:

- Schultz's opportunity came when he joined Starbucks, then a small coffee bean retailer. He envisioned transforming Starbucks into a global coffeehouse chain. Despite initial resistance, Schultz's vision led to the expansion of Starbucks into an international brand with thousands of locations worldwide.

Legacy:

- Schultz's success is a testament to visionary leadership and the ability to scale a business while maintaining its core values. His story emphasizes the importance of innovation and persistence.

4. J.K. Rowling: The Literary Phenomenon

Background:

- Joanne Rowling, known as J.K. Rowling, was born in 1965 in England. She faced significant struggles as a single mother living on welfare before achieving literary success.

Path to Wealth:

- Rowling's journey to wealth began with the creation of the Harry Potter series. Despite numerous rejections from publishers, her perseverance paid off when Bloomsbury Publishing agreed to publish her first book. The series became a global phenomenon, leading to substantial financial success and cultural impact.

Legacy:

- Rowling's rise from poverty to becoming one of the world's wealthiest authors underscores the importance of creativity, resilience, and belief in one's work. Her philanthropy and advocacy work further amplify her influence.

5. Elon Musk: The Tech Innovator

Background:

- Born in 1971 in Pretoria, South Africa, Elon Musk had a tumultuous childhood and faced many challenges. He moved to the United States to pursue higher education and entrepreneurial ambitions.

Path to Wealth:

- Musk's path to wealth involved a series of groundbreaking ventures, including Zip2, PayPal, Tesla, SpaceX, and SolarCity. His innovative approach and willingness to take significant risks have made him one of the most influential figures in technology and space exploration.

Legacy:

- Musk's story highlights the importance of innovation, risk-taking, and relentless pursuit of ambitious goals. His work is transforming industries and shaping the future of technology and space travel.

Conclusion: The Diverse Paths to Wealth

The stories of Andrew Carnegie, Oprah Winfrey, Howard Schultz, J.K. Rowling, and Elon Musk illustrate that there is no single path to wealth. Each individual's journey is unique, shaped by their circumstances, choices, and determination. These stories serve as powerful reminders that resilience, innovation, and perseverance can lead to remarkable financial success, regardless of one's starting point.

In the next chapter, we will examine the environmental and societal costs associated with relentless economic growth, questioning the sustainability of our current financial systems and exploring potential solutions.

CHAPTER 13

THE HIDDEN COSTS OF ECONOMIC GROWTH

Economic growth has long been hailed as a marker of progress and prosperity. However, the relentless pursuit of growth comes with significant environmental and societal costs. This chapter delves into the negative impacts of continuous economic expansion, questioning the sustainability of our current financial systems and exploring potential pathways to a more balanced and equitable future.

Environmental Degradation: The Toll on Nature

1. Climate Change:

   - The industrial activities driving economic growth are major contributors to greenhouse gas emissions, leading to climate change. Rising global temperatures, extreme weather events, and sea-level rise are some of the dire consequences, of threatening ecosystems, human health, and livelihoods.

2. Resource Depletion:

- The extraction and consumption of natural resources, such as fossil fuels, minerals, and forests, have escalated with economic growth. Overexploitation of these resources leads to habitat destruction, loss of biodiversity, and long-term ecological imbalances.

3. Pollution:

- Industrial processes, agricultural practices, and urbanization generate significant pollution, contaminating air, water, and soil. Pollution poses severe health risks to humans and wildlife, affecting quality of life and natural habitats.

Societal Costs: The Human Impact

1. Inequality:

- Economic growth often exacerbates income and wealth inequality. The benefits of growth are disproportionately enjoyed by the wealthy, while marginalized communities struggle to access opportunities and resources, leading to social unrest and instability.

2. Labor Exploitation:

- The demand for cheap labor to fuel economic expansion can lead to exploitative working conditions, including low wages, long hours, and unsafe environments. Child labor and modern slavery are extreme manifestations of this issue.

3. Cultural Erosion:

- Globalization and economic growth can erode local cultures and traditions. The homogenization of cultures driven by consumerism and corporate interests diminishes cultural diversity and weakens community bonds.

The Unsustainability of Current Financial Systems

1. Short-Term Focus:

- The emphasis on short-term financial gains and quarterly earnings reports drives companies to prioritize immediate profits over long-term sustainability. This short-sighted approach often leads to environmental degradation and social injustices.

2. Debt and Financial Instability:

- High levels of debt, both at the individual and national levels, create financial instability. The pressure to service debt can lead to austerity measures, reduced public spending, and economic vulnerability.

3. Overreliance on Growth:

- The current financial system is heavily reliant on continuous economic growth. However, infinite growth is impossible on a finite planet. This reliance creates systemic risks and ignores the limits of natural resources and ecological systems.

Potential Pathways to a Sustainable Future

1. Green Economy:

 - Transitioning to a green economy involves shifting towards sustainable practices that minimize environmental impact. This includes investing in renewable energy, promoting energy efficiency, and adopting circular economy principles to reduce waste.

2. Inclusive Growth:

 - Ensuring that economic growth benefits all members of society requires policies that address inequality and provide opportunities for marginalized communities. This includes fair wages, access to education and healthcare, and social safety nets.

3. Corporate Responsibility:

 - Businesses must adopt sustainable and ethical practices. This includes transparent reporting, reducing carbon footprints, ensuring fair labor practices, and prioritizing social and environmental considerations in decision-making.

4. Policy and Governance:

- Governments play a crucial role in fostering sustainable development. Implementing policies that promote environmental protection, social equity, and economic resilience is essential. This includes regulations, incentives, and international cooperation.

5. Technological Innovation:

- Harnessing technology for sustainability can drive positive change. Innovations in clean energy, sustainable agriculture, and resource-efficient manufacturing can reduce environmental impact and support economic growth.

Conclusion: Balancing Progress and Sustainability

The price of progress, marked by environmental degradation and societal costs, challenges the sustainability of our current financial systems. Achieving a balance between economic growth and sustainability requires a fundamental shift in how we approach development. By prioritizing green economies, inclusive growth, corporate responsibility, and effective governance, we can work towards a future that ensures prosperity for all while preserving the planet for future generations.

In the final chapter, we will speculate on the future of money, considering emerging technologies, alternative economic models, and the potential for a more equitable and sustainable financial future.

CHAPTER 14

THE DISRUPTIVE POWER OF CRYPTOCURRENCIES

The Rise of Digital Currencies

Cryptocurrencies have emerged as a groundbreaking financial innovation with the potential to revolutionize traditional financial systems. Born out of the desire for decentralized and secure digital transactions, cryptocurrencies have rapidly gained popularity and adoption worldwide. This chapter explores the disruptive power of cryptocurrencies, examining their impact on finance, governance, and society.

The Genesis of Cryptocurrencies

1. Bitcoin: The Pioneer:

   - Bitcoin, introduced in 2009 by an anonymous entity known as Satoshi Nakamoto, was the first cryptocurrency. It aimed to create a peer-to-peer electronic cash system that operates without the need for intermediaries like banks. Bitcoin's decentralized nature and the underlying blockchain technology set the stage for a new era of digital finance.

2. Blockchain Technology:

- Blockchain is the foundational technology behind cryptocurrencies. It is a decentralized, distributed ledger that records all transactions across a network of computers. This ensures transparency, security, and immutability, making it resistant to fraud and manipulation.

The Financial Disruption

1. Decentralization:

- Cryptocurrencies operate on decentralized networks, reducing the control and influence of central banks and financial institutions. This decentralization challenges traditional banking systems, offering an alternative means of conducting transactions and storing value.

2. Financial Inclusion:

- Cryptocurrencies have the potential to enhance financial inclusion by providing access to financial services for the unbanked and underbanked populations. Mobile wallets and blockchain-based financial platforms enable individuals in remote and underserved areas to participate in the global economy.

3. Cross-Border Transactions:

- Cryptocurrencies facilitate faster and cheaper cross-border transactions compared to traditional banking methods. This is particularly beneficial for remittances, where high fees and long processing times have been significant barriers.

4. Investment Opportunities:

- The rise of cryptocurrencies has introduced new investment opportunities. Digital assets like Bitcoin and Ethereum have attracted both retail and institutional investors seeking high returns. Cryptocurrency exchanges and trading platforms have proliferated, creating a vibrant ecosystem for digital asset trading.

Challenges to Traditional Finance

1. Regulatory Uncertainty:

- The rapid growth of cryptocurrencies has outpaced regulatory frameworks. Governments and financial regulators are grappling with how to classify, regulate, and tax digital assets. The lack of clear regulations creates uncertainty and poses risks for investors and businesses.

2. Security Concerns:

- While blockchain technology is secure, cryptocurrency exchanges and wallets are vulnerable to hacking and cyberattacks. High-profile hacks, such as the Mt. Gox incident, where millions of dollars' worth of Bitcoin were stolen, highlight the security challenges facing the industry.

3. Market Volatility:

- Cryptocurrencies are known for their price volatility. Dramatic price swings can result in significant gains or losses for investors. This volatility undermines the stability needed for cryptocurrencies to function effectively as a medium of exchange and store of value.

Disruptive Applications Beyond Finance

1. Smart Contracts:

- Smart contracts are self-executing contracts with the terms of the agreement directly written into code. Platforms like Ethereum enable the creation and execution of smart contracts, automating complex transactions and reducing the need for intermediaries in various industries.

2. Decentralized Finance (DeFi):

- DeFi refers to a financial system built on blockchain technology that operates without traditional intermediaries. DeFi platforms offer services such as lending, borrowing, trading, and insurance, democratizing access to financial services and creating new economic opportunities.

3. Tokenization of Assets:

- Blockchain technology allows for the tokenization of physical and digital assets, representing ownership through digital tokens. This process can enhance liquidity, enable fractional ownership, and simplify the transfer of assets like real estate, art, and intellectual property.

4. Digital Identity and Security:

- Cryptocurrencies and blockchain technology offer solutions for digital identity verification and security. Decentralized identity systems can provide individuals with control over their personal data, reducing the risks of identity theft and data breaches.

Social and Political Implications

1. Empowerment and Autonomy:

- Cryptocurrencies empower individuals by providing financial autonomy and reducing dependence on centralized institutions. This can be particularly transformative in regions with unstable currencies or repressive governments.

2. Privacy and Anonymity:

- Cryptocurrencies offer varying degrees of privacy and anonymity in transactions. While this can protect user privacy, it also raises concerns about illicit activities such as money laundering, tax evasion, and financing of terrorism.

3. Government Responses:

- Governments around the world have responded to the rise of cryptocurrencies in different ways. Some have embraced the technology, exploring central bank digital currencies (CBDCs) and blockchain applications, while others have imposed strict regulations or outright bans.

The Future of Cryptocurrencies

1. Mainstream Adoption:

- As awareness and understanding of cryptocurrencies grow, mainstream adoption is likely to increase. Businesses, financial institutions, and consumers are gradually integrating cryptocurrencies into their operations and daily lives.

2. Technological Advancements:

- Ongoing technological advancements in blockchain and cryptocurrencies will address current limitations and unlock new possibilities. Scalability, interoperability, and energy efficiency are key areas of development that will shape the future of the industry.

3. Evolving Regulatory Landscape:

- The regulatory landscape for cryptocurrencies will continue to evolve. Balanced and clear regulations will be crucial for fostering innovation while protecting consumers and ensuring financial stability.

Conclusion: Embracing the Disruption

The disruptive power of cryptocurrencies is reshaping the financial landscape and extending its influence beyond finance into various sectors. While challenges and uncertainties remain, the potential benefits of cryptocurrencies in promoting financial inclusion, enhancing efficiency, and empowering individuals are immense. As we navigate this transformative era, it is essential to embrace the opportunities presented by cryptocurrencies while addressing the associated risks and ethical considerations.

The journey of cryptocurrencies is still unfolding, and their full impact on the global economy and society is yet to be realized. By fostering innovation, collaboration, and responsible regulation, we can harness the disruptive power of cryptocurrencies to create a more inclusive, efficient, and equitable financial system for the future.

CHAPTER 15

THE FUTURE OF FINANCE

A New Horizon for Money

As we stand at the cusp of a new era, the future of finance is being shaped by rapid technological advancements, evolving economic models, and a growing awareness of the need for sustainability and equity. This chapter explores the potential directions money and financial systems might take, considering the transformative power of innovation and the quest for a more inclusive and sustainable future.

Emerging Technologies Transforming Finance

1. Blockchain and Cryptocurrencies:

 - Blockchain technology offers a decentralized and transparent way to record transactions, reducing the need for intermediaries and enhancing security. Cryptocurrencies like Bitcoin and Ethereum are pioneering this space, offering alternatives to traditional currencies. These digital assets could revolutionize cross-border transactions, reduce transaction costs, and empower individuals in regions with unstable banking systems.

2. Central Bank Digital Currencies (CBDCs):

- Central banks around the world are exploring the development of their own digital currencies. CBDCs aim to combine the benefits of digital transactions with the stability of traditional currencies. They have the potential to improve monetary policy efficiency, enhance financial inclusion, and reduce the risks associated with private cryptocurrencies.

3. Artificial Intelligence and Machine Learning:

- AI and machine learning are transforming financial services through improved risk assessment, fraud detection, and personalized financial advice. These technologies enable more accurate predictions and efficient operations, enhancing the customer experience and reducing costs.

4. Decentralized Finance (DeFi):

- DeFi platforms leverage blockchain technology to offer financial services without traditional intermediaries. These platforms provide lending, borrowing, trading, and investing opportunities in a decentralized manner, promoting greater financial inclusion and accessibility.

Alternative Economic Models

1. Circular Economy:

  - The circular economy model focuses on sustainability by promoting the reuse, repair, and recycling of products. This approach minimizes waste and encourages resource efficiency, creating new economic opportunities while protecting the environment.

2. Social and Solidarity Economy:

  - This model emphasizes social goals and community well-being over profit maximization. It includes cooperatives, social enterprises, and community-based organizations that prioritize social and environmental impact, fostering a more equitable economic system.

3. Universal Basic Income (UBI):

  - UBI is a proposed economic model where all citizens receive a regular, unconditional sum of money from the government. This approach aims to reduce poverty, enhance economic security, and provide a safety net in an era of increasing automation and job displacement.

4. Sustainable Finance:

- Sustainable finance integrates environmental, social, and governance (ESG) criteria into financial decision-making. By prioritizing investments that contribute to sustainability, this approach supports long-term economic growth while addressing global challenges like climate change and inequality.

The Potential for a More Equitable and Sustainable Future

1. Financial Inclusion:

- Emerging technologies and innovative financial models can enhance financial inclusion by providing access to banking and financial services for underserved populations. Mobile banking, digital wallets, and microfinance are examples of solutions that empower individuals and small businesses.

2. Ethical and Responsible Investing:

- The rise of impact investing and ESG-focused funds reflects a growing demand for ethical and responsible investment options. Investors are increasingly seeking to align their portfolios with their values, driving positive social and environmental outcomes.

3. Collaborative Consumption:

- The sharing economy promotes collaborative consumption, where individuals share access to goods and services, reducing waste and increasing resource efficiency. Platforms like Airbnb, Uber, and peer-to-peer lending exemplify this trend, fostering a more sustainable economic model.

4. Policy and Regulation:

- Governments and regulatory bodies play a critical role in shaping the future of finance. Effective policies and regulations can promote innovation, protect consumers, and ensure that financial systems contribute to broader societal goals. International cooperation will be essential to address global challenges and create a fair and resilient financial landscape.

5. Education and Literacy:

- Enhancing financial literacy and education is vital for empowering individuals to make informed financial decisions. Access to knowledge and resources can help people navigate the complexities of modern finance and participate more fully in the economic system.

Conclusion: Embracing the Future

The future of finance holds immense potential for transformation and progress. By leveraging emerging technologies, adopting alternative economic models, and prioritizing sustainability and equity, we can build a financial system that supports a prosperous and inclusive future for all. The journey ahead will require collaboration, innovation, and a commitment to balancing economic growth with the well-being of society and the planet.

As we close this exploration of money and its many facets, we are reminded that the true power of wealth lies not just in its accumulation but in its capacity to drive positive change and create a better world for future generations.

CONCLUSION

Conclusion: The Multifaceted Power of Money

Money, in all its forms and functions, wields immense power that shapes economies, societies, and individual lives. Its ability to drive growth, create wealth, and facilitate transactions underscores its fundamental role in modern civilization. However, money's influence extends far beyond its practical uses, impacting social structures, political dynamics, and ethical considerations.

Economic Growth and Development:

Money is a critical engine of economic growth and development. It enables investment, drives innovation, and enhances productivity. From the early days of barter systems to the complex financial markets of today, the evolution of money has facilitated unprecedented levels of trade and economic expansion. Financial instruments and markets allow for the efficient allocation of resources, supporting businesses and fostering entrepreneurship. The availability of capital is essential for the development of infrastructure, education, healthcare, and technology, all of which contribute to improving living standards and reducing poverty.

Wealth Creation and Inequality:

While money can generate immense wealth, it can also exacerbate inequality. The concentration of wealth in the hands of a few individuals and corporations often leads to significant economic and social disparities. Access to capital and investment opportunities is not evenly distributed, creating barriers to economic mobility for many. This inequality can manifest in various ways, including wage gaps, unequal access to education and healthcare, and limited opportunities for marginalized communities. Addressing these disparities requires a combination of progressive policies, inclusive economic practices, and robust social safety nets.

Social and Political Influence:

Money's power extends into the social and political realms, influencing governance, policy-making, and social structures. Political campaigns and policy decisions are often heavily influenced by financial contributions and lobbying efforts. This can lead to regulatory capture, where industries manipulate regulations to their advantage, often at the expense of public interest. Additionally, the ability of wealthy individuals and organizations to shape public discourse and political outcomes raises questions about the fairness and integrity of democratic processes.

Technological and Environmental Impact:

The relationship between money and technology is symbiotic, with financial resources driving technological advancements and innovations reshaping financial systems. Emerging technologies, such as blockchain and cryptocurrencies, are disrupting traditional financial models and creating new opportunities and challenges. At the same time, the pursuit of economic growth has significant environmental implications. Industrial activities, resource extraction, and consumerism contribute to environmental degradation and climate change. Balancing economic development with environmental sustainability is one of the most pressing challenges of our time.

Ethical Considerations:

The ethical dimensions of money involve its use, distribution, and the values it promotes. The pursuit of profit can sometimes lead to unethical practices, such as exploitation, corruption, and environmental harm. Ensuring that financial activities align with broader social and ethical values is crucial for building a just and sustainable economy. This includes promoting transparency, accountability, and corporate social responsibility.

The Future of Money:

The future of money is being shaped by rapid technological advancements, evolving economic models, and a growing emphasis on sustainability and equity. Digital currencies, decentralized finance, and innovative financial technologies are transforming how we think about and interact with money. These changes hold the promise of greater financial inclusion, efficiency, and empowerment. However, they also pose new risks and challenges that require careful consideration and management.

Embracing the Potential of Money Responsibly:

The power of money is a double-edged sword, capable of driving both progress and devastation. To harness its potential responsibly, we must address the inequalities it can create, ensure that financial systems are inclusive and transparent, and align economic activities with ethical and environmental considerations. By fostering a balanced approach to money, we can leverage its power to build a more equitable, sustainable, and prosperous future for all.

As we navigate the complexities of the modern financial landscape, it is essential to remember that money is a tool, not an end in itself. Its true value lies in its ability to improve lives, support communities, and create opportunities. By understanding and managing the multifaceted power of money, we can ensure that it serves the greater good and contributes to a more just and thriving world.

Power of Money

www.ingramcontent.com/pod-product-compliance
Lightning Source LLC
Chambersburg PA
CBHW052327220526
45472CB00001B/307